Canadian Animals
Wolverines

Sandra McIntyre

Weigl

Published by Weigl Educational Publishers Limited
6325 10th Street S.E.
Calgary, Alberta T2H 2Z9

www.weigl.com
Canadian Animals series © 2011
Weigl Educational Publishers Limited

Library and Archives Canada Cataloguing in Publication
McIntyre, Sandra, 1970-
             Wolverines / Sandra McIntyre.

(Canadian animals)
Includes index.
Issued also in electronic format.
ISBN 978-1-55388-671-6 (bound).–ISBN 978-1-55388-672-3
(pbk.)

1. Wolverine–Canada–Juvenile literature.
I. Title. II. Series: Canadian animals (Calgary, Alta.)

QL737.C25M34 2010 j599.76'6C2009-907377-3

Editor
Josh Skapin
Design
Terry Paulhus

Photograph Credits
Every reasonable effort has been made to trace ownership and
to obtain permission to reprint copyright material. The publishers
would be pleased to have any errors or omissions brought to
their attention so that they may be corrected in
subsequent printings.

Weigl acknowledges Getty Images as one of its primary image
suppliers for this title.

Alamy: page 5
Dreamstime: pages 17, 19, 22
Peter Arnold: pages 4, 10, 12, 20

We gratefully acknowledge the financial support of the
Government of Canada through the Canada Book Fund for our
publishing activities.

Printed in United States of America in North Mankata, Minnesota
1 2 3 4 5 6 7 8 9 0 14 13 12 11 10

062010
WEP230610

Contents

Meet the Wolverine

Wolverines are **mammals** that look like small bears. They have long claws, large paws, and thick brown fur. Wolverines live in places that have cold weather.

Many people believe wolverines are closely related to the wolf. This is not true. Wolverines belong to the weasel family. Weasels are **predators** with long bodies and short legs.

▼ Wolverines can live up to 10 years in nature.

Wolverine Facts

- Wolverines are sometimes called skunk bears because they have stripes on their bodies. Skunks also have stripes.

- Wolverines are the largest members of the weasel family.

▲ Baby wolverines are called kits.

A Very Special Animal

Wolverines are powerful animals. They have strong legs to help them run from enemies. The wolverine's legs are also used for climbing.

Wolverines climb trees to escape danger. They also climb trees to hide food or wait for **prey**.

▶ Wolverines may hide in trees and jump down on top of their prey.

Thick fur keeps
frost off the
wolverine's body.

Wolverines have sharp
teeth that they use to
tear frozen prey.

Wolverines have long
claws for climbing
and digging.

Where Do They Live?

Wolverines live in North America, Europe, and Asia. In Canada, wolverines are found in most provinces and territories.

A **range** is a section of land where the wolverine will hunt for food. The wolverine's range is large. Males have a range of about 620 kilometres. Females have a smaller range between 130 and 260 kilometres.

▶ Wolverines live in forests and grasslands.

Wolverine Range

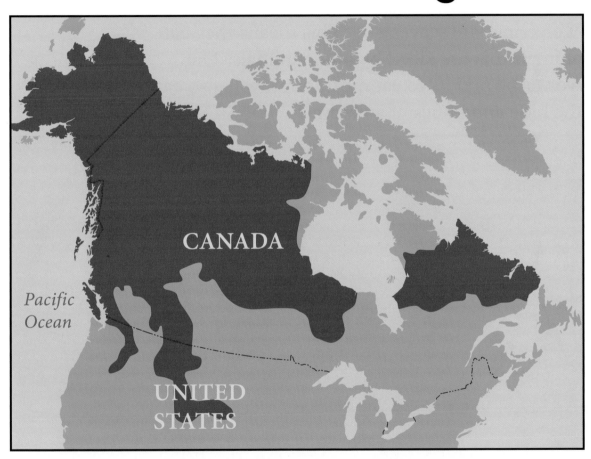

CANADA

Pacific
Ocean

UNITED
STATES

N
W · E
S

0   500 Miles
0   500 Kilometers

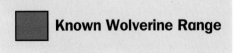

Known Wolverine Range

What Do They Eat?

Wolverines are scavengers. This means they eat animals that are killed by other animals. The wolverine prefers to eat meat, but it will also eat the hide and bones of an animal.

▼ Hungry wolverines will steal food from other animals.

What a Meal!

Wolverines sometimes hunt small animals when they cannot find food to scavenge. These are some of the animals they hunt.

- mice
- squirrels
- geese
- hares
- porcupines

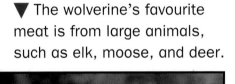

▼ The wolverine's favourite meat is from large animals, such as elk, moose, and deer.

Living Alone

Wolverines prefer to live alone. They search for places to live where there are no other wolverines.

One of the few times wolverines live together is when a mother has kits. Kits live in a **den** with their mother. When kits are about seven months old, they begin looking for food by themselves.

◀ The only other time wolverines live together is during mating season.

Wolverine Talk

Most wolverines communicate by marking their territory. They have scent glands that produce a strong odour. Wolverines mark their territory by rubbing against trees. The odour left behind warns other wolverines to stay away.

▲ Wolverines may grunt or growl to communicate.

Growing Up

Most female wolverines give birth to two or three kits at a time. Kits are born in a den between February and May.

Wolverines build dens in hollow trees, caves, or tunnels in the snow. A mother wolverine may have several dens. She will move kits often to keep them safe from predators.

▼ Wolverine kits are full grown by the time they reach seven months old.

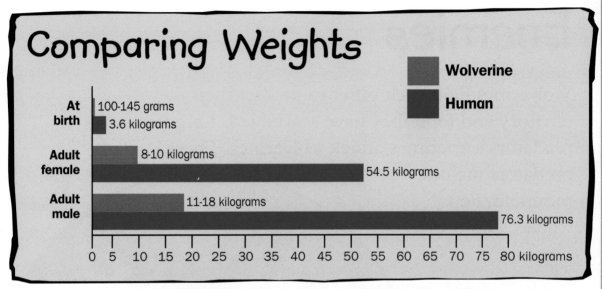

Comparing Weights

Wolverine
Human

	Wolverine	Human
At birth	100-145 grams	3.6 kilograms
Adult female	8-10 kilograms	54.5 kilograms
Adult male	11-18 kilograms	76.3 kilograms

0 5 10 15 20 25 30 35 40 45 50 55 60 65 70 75 80 kilograms

▶ Wolverines rarely have kits two years in a row.

Enemies

Wolverines fight each other to protect their territory and food they have scavenged. Large predators sometimes attack wolverines. These predators include mountain lions, wolves, and bears.

▶ Wolves compete with wolverines for the same kinds of food.

Comparing Sizes

Wolverines fluff their fur, raise their tail, and growl at enemies. These animals have been known to chase away animals that are much larger in size. Bears and wolves are two examples.

Bear

Wolf

Wolverine

Under Threat

Humans are the biggest threat to wolverines. At one time, wolverines lived in most parts of Canada. However, the wolverine population in eastern Canada has decreased in recent years. This may be due to hunting.

Wolverines are hunted for their fur. Wolverine fur is brown with two stripes of yellow down the sides. Some people use the fur for clothing.

▼ Wolverine fur can be used to make mittens and moccasins.

▲ Wolverine fur is used to make clothing, such as jackets. This is because wolverine fur does not stay wet for long.

What Do You Think?

Over time, hunting by humans could become a threat to the wolverine population. Should wolverines be protected by law from hunters? Should people continue to hunt wolverines for their fur?

Myths and Legends

Storytelling is important to First Nations. Many of Canada's First Nations tell stories about the wolverine.

In one Innu story, a wolverine named Kuekuatsheu was near a river when he noticed the water rising. He moved away from the water and was soon on top of a mountain. The water continued to rise, so Kuekuatsheu built a raft. As Kuekuatsheu floated on the raft, he saw other animals were frightened by the rising water. The wolverine asked the other animals to bring him rocks and mud. He used the mud and rocks to build a safe place for the other animals to escape the rising water. This is how Kuekuatsheu made the land people live on today.

▶ Some First Nations legends see the wolverine as a magical creature.

The wolverine is nicknamed "glutton." Glutton is a term used to describe someone who eats too much. The wolverine eats as much as it can. This is because the wolverine never knows when it will find food.

In the X-men comic books, there is a character named Wolverine. He is a **mutant** man with claws that can be drawn in. Actor Hugh Jackman plays the role of Wolverine in the X-Men movies.

▶ Hugh Jackman has played Wolverine in four movies. In 2009, he won a Teen Choice award for *X-Men Origins: Wolverine*.

Quiz

1. Which family does the wolverine belong to?
   (*a*) **bear** (*b*) **wolf** (*c*) **weasel**

2. Where do wolverines live?
   (*a*) **in hot places** (*b*) **in deserts** (*c*) **in cold places**

3. What are baby wolverines called?
   (*a*) **pups** (*b*) **kits** (*c*) **calves**

4. Which of these animals may attack wolverines?
   (*a*) **blue jays** (*b*) **mountain lions** (*c*) **chipmunks**

Answers:

1. (c) The wolverine belongs to the weasel family.
2. (c) Wolverines live in cold places.
3. (b) Baby wolverines are called kits.
4. (b) Mountain lions may attack wolverines.

Find out More

To find out more about wolverines, you can write to these organizations or visit their websites.

World Wildlife Fund, Canada
245 Eglinton Avenue East
Suite 410
Toronto, Ontario
M4P 3J1
www.wwf.ca

Wildlife Conservation Society Canada
Suite 600
720 Spadina Avenue
Toronto, Ontario
M5S 2T9
www.wcs.org

Words to Know

den
an animal's home; usually for looking after young

mammals
animals that have hair or fur and feed milk to their young

mutant
an organism that has a body different from others in its species

predators
animals that hunt other animals for food

prey
an animal that is hunted for food

range
the area where an animal lives

Index